An Alpha Male's Love

Reighn

PAGE PUBLISHING
Conneaut Lake, PA

First originally published by Page Publishing 2023

ISBN 979-8-88654-011-6 (pbk)
ISBN 979-8-88654-015-4 (digital)

Printed in the United States of America

This book is dedicated to my family, friends, loved ones, as well as my GrandBuds and my CWG sister. All of you have taught me to use life to an advantage. I'll be screaming, "Colored white girl forever!"

When men refer to themselves as "Alpha Males", I hear that in context of software, where Alpha versions are unstable, missing important features, filled with flaws, and not fit for the public.

—Glenn F. Henriksen

Day Mares

Every morning I wake, I feel as if I've left behind a piece of myself.
I feel trapped, I'm discouraged, and I'm in need of a lot of help.
Daily, I feel as if my soul has abandoned my outer shell.
My personality is deteriorating, my life is becoming a living hell.
I'm starting to feel out of place in this world, in this life.
I feel that there's nothing more that I can do to end this horrible fight…

Explanation of Reighn

My homegirl read some of my poems one day. She looked at me, shocked, and said, "Girl, what's wrong? Are you okay?"

She said my writings made her feel sad and somewhat depressed. She wondered if suicide was the only choice that I had left. I said no! I had two choices: either life or death, so I chose to write in order to make peace between the devil and myself. The way I see it, my writings are my therapy. As I expanded my mental, I learned that I could take care of me! If I had not started to write as of this day, I wouldn't know exactly where I would be.

I mean, I had to find another way to deal with these happy but yet troubled visions I see. So in my reality, I have committed suicide. It's in my mind, and it no longer has a trivial place to hide.

Speaking to My Reflection

Ooh, I guess that's why you think that I don't believe in you. Honestly, it's only you that I do believe in, not anyone else. I have more faith in you, because you are the only one that I see.

Females, Break the Chain

Does love really make females that damn stupid?
If it does, someone needs to smack the hell out of cupid.
When will females open their eyes to see,
that sex objects are usually all they will ever be.
'Cause a female's self-esteem can sink very low,
if the d——k is the only thing that they choose to grow.
How much more disrespect will most females keep
putting up with?
The disrespect alone should literally make us as females sick.

When females are involved in relationships where
the situation tends to remain the same
there should leave no room for those females to open
their mouths to ever complain.
Especially if those females keep believing every alpha male's lame excuse;
putting up with obvious shit; and taking the mental abuse.
Females, we have to be the ones to break the chains,
we can't keep letting alpha males mess up our good names.

When females learn that they don't have to jump
to serve an alpha male's every command.
Females will gain pride in themselves!
Females will take a stand!
I'm desperate to help all females out of this deceitful way of life,
females, please pay attention…here's my slice of life's advice…

Sex shouldn't be confused as love,
please get it right,
Ecstasy should last a lifetime,
not just for one night.

Untitled

It felt so familiar…when you pressed
your lips to mine.
It was like running in slow
motion as the hands moved
backwards in time.
I was placed back to the point when
I kissed my first dude.
The moment was so
right…I was feeling the mood…
For a second or two, it was like
my whole body went under a trance.
I was like butter pecan ice cream…
I melted and left my nuts drippin'
in his hands.
I was overwhelmed,
'cause it was something I felt once before,
that tingle in my hormones that screams,
"Give me more! Give me more!"
Not wanting to open my eyes to view
my present sight,
If enjoyin' him is wrong,
will imagining him make it right?

Change of Heart

When I look in your eyes it feels strange,
maybe it's because my feelings for you have changed.
The only memory in your eyes I see,
is the day that you walked out on me.
I never thought that day would come,
now I see that thought…well, it was dumb.
All the hell I put you through now it's out of spite,
'cause you walked out on me that night.
I'm sorry that's the only image that my mind's eye can see,
but you promised me that you would never leave.
I wish things could go back to being the
same ol' same,
but my old feelings…they no longer remain.
And since my mind can't seem to see
beyond that sight,
I'll be alright, if you walk out on me tonight…

My 2 Weeks' Notice

I'M FINALLY LEAVIN' THIS JOB
'CAUSE I'M INCORRECTLY PRICED,
AFTER WORKIN' HARD 2 PAY MY BILLS,
MY POCKETS DON'T FEEL 2 NICE.

THIS PLACE IS MAKIN' IT HARDER
AND HARDER 4 ME TO GET OUT THE BED EVERY DAY,
AS SOON AS MY TOES TOUCH THE FLOOR,
I INSTANTLY BEGIN 2 PRAY.

I'M TIRED OF ALL THE BULLSHIT
CIRCLIN' AROUND MY HEAD,
I'M BEGINNING 2 ENVISION AT LEAST
1 OF MY RESIDENTS DEAD.

I'VE PUT UP WITH MORE A$$HOLES
THAN I CAN DEAL WITH,
IF THE DIRECTOR OF NURSING
HAPPENS 2 PASS BY,
I'LL LOOK HER IN HER FACE AND SPIT!

BUT IT'S OKAY THOUGH,
'CAUSE AFTER THESE 2 WEEKS,
MY SCRUBS I WILL GLADLY RETIRE,
INSTEAD OF ME, IT'S YOU
THAT'S BEIN' TOLD "YOU'RE FIRED!"

Peace of Mind

ONE LAST POEM, NOW THE PRESSURE IS ON ME,
THE TOPIC IS SUPPOSED TO BE ABOUT SOMETHING
FUNNY, BUT I DON'T FEEL LIKE LAUGHING.
AT THIS POINT IN TIME, I'M NOT FEELING THE MOOD,
WITH EVERY WORD I WRITE, I'M
CATCHING AN ATTITUDE.
MY HAPPINESS IS BEING HELD CAPTIVE WAY
IN THE BACK OF THE VAULT,
TO WRITE FUNNY NOW WOULD BE AN INSULT.
MY HUMOUROUS STORIES ARE NOT BEING GRANTED
TOTAL CLEARANCE,
THERE'S HOSTILE TURMOIL THAT'S INSINUATING
INTERFERENCE.
MY BRAIN CAN'T SEEM TO MAKE MY PENCIL
REACH ANOTHER ERECTION,
'CAUSE MY HEART KNOWS MY WORDS DON'T
SHOW PROOF OF AFFECTION.
HOWEVER, IN A FEW DAYS, IM SURE I'LL GAIN THAT
WARM, FUZZY FEELING THAT I USED TO KNOW BACK,
BUT RIGHT NOW, I NEED TO TAKE THIS TIME TO
REGROUP AND RELAX…

My 1st Tennessee Rain

…Sittin' in front of my windowpane
watching my 1st Tennessee rain.
I was listenin' to the sound as the rain hit the pavement,
I reflected on how much lovemakin' in it would be an amazement.
The sweet smell of my 1st Tennessee rain
made me close my eyes and draw a picture in my brain.
…I thought of how sexy it would be to have him here, right here
    sexin' me.
He would hold me close and kiss my lips, as he would rub his hands
    up and down my hips.
Now holdin' my hands as we are on the balcony,
I would lift one leg and he would push his love inside me.
My moans would be like my favorite singer singin' over the beat of
    my 1st Tennessee rain,
his hypnotic…rhythmic…motions, yes…ooh, yes, I came.
He would then put my leg back on the ground, he would kiss me
    again
and turn my naked body around.
He would then enter me with his love from the back,
makin' me call his name and moan more with every tap.
A few more strokes…then another position we would change,
as our lovemakin' continued in my 1st Tennessee rain.
I would sit on his lap as he would play with my clit,
one…two…three, his rubber duckie got sick.
We would hold each other even after we both came,
still sittin' outside on the balcony in my 1st Tennessee rain…

Nightmares

I go to sleep
in a cold, lonely; unstable bed.
I shake, I shiver,
I throw the covers over my head.
I cry out to my Creator,
I beg him to take me beyond this
place. My state of mind is fragile,
I'm losing hope in fate.
I've disappointed myself again;
I whisper as the tears roll
down my face. There's no help
for me now. I'm afraid it's over…
it's too late.

An Alpha Male's Love

He teaches her. He shows her, her weaknesses. He understands her strengths and pushes her as hard and as far as the fuck he can… He's an alpha male. He doesn't know when to shut up. He doesn't know when to let go. He has all the solutions to any problem. Yep, you've guessed it…he's an alpha male. He's patient, but he overindulges in competition. He possesses unchecked aggression. He's careless, and at the same time, he restrains his heart, leaving her soul abandoned and her spirit unfulfilled. She's unknowing to what true form of his love he will reveal. The life has literally been sucked out of their relationship. It used to be when they left each other or came back home, there would be small pink lips awaiting to greet his full brown lips with sweet and gentle kisses. Now those days are long, long gone.

"It's been at least two or three years since he ran his soft pudgy fingertips over my luminous golden skin," is something she would say. "And who knows when the last time or how long it's been since I've fathomed my alpha male's scent." Instinctively, frustration made her sick when she realized that her dreams of her alpha male were not quite as often anymore. She immediately begins to give up on him, but her alpha male is there making sure that she won't.

He caresses her arms nervously, looking at her through his glassy dark brown eyes. He clears his thin dry throat. His voice is subtle yet commanding as his vocal cords allows him to speak to her. "Think with me and not against me," something he would usually say when he felt that their glue wasn't holding together their bond. He's stroking her short thick hair while he's pressing her head lightly against his broad but hairless chest. He holds her tight in his long, skinny cut arms. His reaction was to pull her closer when she trembled from the vibrations and pace of his heart's beat. He's an alpha male. He doesn't accept defeat.

He quickly recognizes his inhuman flaws as he begins to analyze, compound, and comprehend the equity that they've shared throughout their revolving relationship. He starts to suppress his selfishness and pettiness that consumes him no longer.

As for her, she holds her head high as she breathes deep because she has been shown that there are real signs in life, like the ones that show through as relief. Much like her alpha male, she understands that he needs her to need him. The pressure from a stalled, strained relationship has finally been lifted in the course of one night. For now, she's not afraid of his love, and she doesn't run from his much-needed attention.

Stoic Woman

I'm a little afraid to run with these thoughts, but I speak the truth. I have never been the one to play by the rules in relationships. I've tackled each as if they were games, making every one a victory. As the star performer in these situations, I was always seen socializing happily accepting the attention until I met him. Now, I'm in the middle of now, where he became the life that I wasn't aware of. His relentless effort broke down the resistance to my charm and I responded by taking action prematurely. In the past, I was in control. I trusted my perceptions, but his talents and courtesies proved to be superior to a stoic woman's style. I can't believe I let his mood overpower me. I was becoming increasingly skeptical of my surroundings. My comfort zone had been disrupted and I felt as if I could no longer function in my environment. I became a woman scorned, but I was not fed up.

You must fight for your freedom, my subconscious spoke to me as I stared in the mirror over the bathroom sink with tears in my eyes and nostrils flaring. I pulled my hair into a messy ponytail that sat on top of my head, lit some candles, and started a bath. As I soaked in the hot water, I had my eyes closed and head bowed submissively because I was feeling sorry for myself. I suddenly felt a cold wind come from the door being opened. When I opened my eyes, there he was, sitting on the edge of the tub, pawing at the water, looking at me with frustration on his face.

"What's your problem?" he said calmly. His boldness surprised me.

My response was sharp. "I'm resenting the fact that I'm in this relationship." His expression went from frustration to disgust. I continued nervously, "No seriously, I feel weak. I envy the person I've become. I never used to worry about us or our family, but since all we ever do is argue, I see us separate, and it's discouraging."

"What?" he said softly. "We're human, but you can't let the conflict between the past and present defeat us. We've come too far. I'm not going anywhere," he said as he prepares to leave the bathroom, "But you deserve to have what it is you want. I just hope you realize what you have when you're making your decision."

The door closed and I was alone again.

You can't predict your life, but you do control it. That little voice in my head was back.

"I hate it when he's right," I screamed and reached for my apple blossom/shea butter–scented body wash.

On my way to my room, I admitted to myself that I was tired, tired of everything going wrong. I just wanted to sleep 'cause nothing ever went wrong when I was sleeping.

It was midday when I awoke and I insisted upon being delighted. I couldn't settle for mediocre pleasure on this warm spring afternoon. "No sir, not today," I spoke proudly, as I rinsed the foamy toothpaste down the drain.

I was feeling a need for noble, unimpeachable pleasure, so I ran over to my walk-in closet, swung open the door, grabbed my red spaghetti-string back-out shirt, my form-fitting Polo jeans with the red, white, and blue slits on the sides, slipped into my red tweed heels, spiked my hair in the front, glanced over at myself one last time, and headed for the door. I also decided to leave my car in the driveway and I walked.

To keep a short story short, I didn't get fifty yards before some light-skinned guy in a gray 2006 Nissan Titan truck came to a halt in front of me. He let his window down.

"What's a beautiful individual like yourself doing walking? Where's your man?"

"Thanks," I said with wide eyes and a huge smile.

Shooting back a bright smile, he replied, "Would you except a ride to wherever it is you're going?"

"Sure," I said, keeping my smile. "As long as you drop me back at this spot." Now I'm not advising that you get in the car with every person who just so happens to stop, but a stoic woman knows her world, and I knew the faster the mission was completed, the better.

In the truck, we discussed the facts. "Yes, my man and I are happy, yes, I'm truly half your age, and no, I won't be calling you, but definitely thanks for the ride."

Once I returned home, there was a note stuck to the door in all caps that read, "HAVE YOU MADE YOUR CHOICE?"

Stunned for the second time by his actions, I ran into the house yelling his name and finding him nowhere. As I was placing my shoes back in their box, I heard the faint sound of music coming from the bathroom. I listened until I recognized that the song was one that we had worked together on. Walking and singing along, I pushed open the door to see that he was waiting for me.

"My choice!" I said, with happy tears streaming down my face. "My choice is always my family." He tried to respond, but I told him, "There was no need." He then kissed me gently and pointed toward the tub.

It was almost midnight when I said, "I bought you something earlier," and handed him a silver paperweight with a quote that read, "A journey of a thousand miles begins with a single step. —Confucius." He laughed and put his arms around me and said simply, "I agree to agree."

Still in the Game

Love and sex have nothing to do with each other, but if you have great love, you will always have great sex. An unknown quote that grazed the prominent mustached lips of a tenuous, kind-natured man as his deep brown eyes focused upon a message that had been left on the dusty mirror of the Key Motel that read, "*Pretty and pink, gives great head, and takes ass shots like no other…for another excellent romp, dial me soon…–Kisses.*"

His reflection flashed his straight pearly whites as he recalled the scenes that had taken place a few hours ago. Wishing she was still lying next to him, he opened his eyes, air-kissed her back, gathered his clothing, and retired to the shower.

"Vanity Knightingale" was her stripper name, he reminisced as her juices streamed down his leg into the drain. She was a sophisticated possession that he had been cheating with for about four or five years now. The two moved their relationship outside the strip club and into every cheap motel they could find three months into their meetings.

He has had numerous flings over the years, but, Vanity…Vanity was the first one who took him to *space*—that *special place* where *all cum eternally.* She was a "perfect opposite," he said as he remembered licking her honey-sweet skin and groping her firm C-cup breast, all while he was watching her apple-bottom booty bounce, wiggle, and jiggle in the air. As the water continued to pulsate and bead against his forty-two-inch dark chocolate muscular back, his left hand found his erect manhood, as his right hand became a brace, holding on to the shower pole, allowing him to reenact the whole hour and twenty minutes he spent with her in just a matter of minutes

The hot water turned cold as he washed the mannish smirk off his face. "It is what it is," he said, grinning as he shut the water off, wrapped a towel around himself, and exited the bathroom.

Leaving the keys and a twenty-dollar tip for the desk clerk, he walked casually out to his custom glossy charcoal-gray *2007 Impala SS*, retracted the hard top, revved the engine, and drove southbound, anticipating their next meeting.

At home already, Vanity was sitting on the couch with her eyes closed, listening to the *Maury Povich Show* while she practiced how to write from pure thought without looking at the page when an unwelcome presence appeared.

"Are you all right?"

"No," Vanity replied with bitterness in her voice, "I lost my train of thought."

"Look at you, *Ms.* Poet by Night and Stripper by Midnight," he said, trying to pull a laugh out of her.

Heat rose to her cheeks. "Ooh, how so not funny," she said as she stood up, knocking her papers to the floor. "What exactly are you trying to imply with a comment like that?"

Confusion took over his eyes as he replied, "All I expected was a laugh, since it's such a rare thing between us lately. You're becoming…more and more…stubborn."

Her ears hung on his last word. As she stomped halfway up the stairs, she turned and hissed back to him, "I gotta get ready for work."

The thunderous bass from the song "Sex Games" by R&B artist Case shook her emotions when she walked through the glass doors of club Genitalia. She sang along, *"Is it too late to come on over and play sex games…"*

The DJ gave her an explicit look and she gave him the middle finger when she passed by his booth on her way to the Divas' Quarters. Walking past other female employees, Vanity batted her long natural eyelashes on her ageless face, faked a gentle yet bold smile as she shimmied her tight golden ass across the room to her dressing booth. There she noticed a red-and-yellow Gloriosa lily in front of a small sterling silver book stand that held a first-edition autographed copy of Michael Baisden's book, *Men Cry in the Dark*. Her head tilted with compassion as she plucked the book from its gorgeous stand and rubbed two fingers in awe over Michael Baisden's signed name. Her emotions immediately checked themselves when she understood that her preferred partner was going to be somewhere lurking in the crowd.

All eyes focused center stage as the lights went dim. Vanity was perched on a stool wearing sleek black stiletto thigh-high boots, a black onyx thong and bra set, with a shirt made from shredded pieces of an unidentifiable football team jersey.

The sirens from her song selection rang out as the intro began, "Yeah...*I-I-I can see that ass from the front of it...*" Her curved hips started to sway as she stood to reveal her valuable assets to her non-valued onlookers. Money came from all directions when she performed a memorable pole movement that ended the song as well as her performance. Delighted, Vanity collected her money, bowed in thanks, and exited the stage.

Unballing, as well as counting her money, Vanity placed a stack of fives, tens, and ones in front of her most recent gift. She stared lovingly at the title and admitted that her aliment was, there was a struggle between what she preferred and what she felt. She was tired of going home to have sex with someone just to get her rocks off. Vanity had fallen in love with the come-and-go part of her preferred relationship. Around him, her feelings were free. She was able to explore, which influenced her sex drive. She knew that after tonight, she could not be the same person she was in the beginning.

She started to speak, "Besides, going home to a nonaffectioned person who..." Her thoughts were interrupted by a kiss on the back of her neck that snapped her back to reality.

"It's raining outside," a baritone voice spoke in her ear. Her spot was marked. She became moist as she reached for her umbrella. The two proceeded to their separate vehicles for they knew their saga would continue.

Won't Be Very Long

But it's not going to be the same for us this time. I'm not going to leave you. We will raise her together. Just please don't make… make me give up our baby. We knew the consequence of having premeditated unprotected sex. And we knew that there were plenty of methods we should have used to avoid this pregnancy, but yet, I am pregnant. And I agreed to an abortion due to you solely complaining about your age and the two us already having three grown children between us, but please, please don't make me hold true to that. Our growing fetus will soon be born unto us as our baby, our child, our little girl. God has sent us a whimsical conceptus. He has blessed us with a symbol of us, and I'm pleading to hear her cry, to listen to her a voice. I feel her deep within me, in my soul; I feel her. I know this time the Lord has blessed us with a beautiful baby girl, our very own sweet little baby girl. She's our angel, and I would like to introduce our angel, our daughter, into this world as…Cuemie (Q-my), our blossoming butterfly, our sight, the joy of our day.

Clear happiness, our virtue, I can picture her. Can you? Can you see her, our flesh, our blood, with two or three pigtails in her hair, with heart-shaped hair ties securing each end, the back of her yellow shirt waving around as she rides her pink bike up and down our street's hills. Her little round face appears scrunched up in determination as she walks her pink bike back up the hills. Then, as if she were fast as lighting, she'd be off, her little legs pedaling faster and faster as she rides her pink bike back down the hills. I visualize her with her mind's eye open because she believes she is somehow faster than the wind.

Ooh, I can see her tiny hands folded together as she kneels beside her bed. We're standing watching over her in the doorway as she recites her day and nighttime prayers. My goodness, if only I could release some of this joy from inside of me and impose it on you. I can't ignore her. I want to be able to feel her tiny feet kick back from within every time her daddy decides to take the time out from his busy day to give her mommy's tummy a quick pity pat. I dream, I often dream, of myself as a volunteer chaperone for her high school's school bus. We'd laugh, cry, and sing rowdily together as we road back and forth across country to become participants in college campus walking tours. I can't, I simply cannot take your request seriously. You couldn't possibly still want me to go through with this. I'm lost. Look me in my eyes and tell me that witnessing your grandchildren's homecoming celebration is something that you're honestly aiming to miss. Please don't believe that I've acquired an obvious understanding at this point. Your request is still unclear. What you're expecting of me just isn't getting through.

I can judge by that perplexed expression upon your face, you are still refusing to view the life of your child, our daughter, as a win. The odds are in our favor. I don't want to hear any more elaborate excuses. Will you believe through your doubt that our finances are no longer a part of this equation, rather than use the amounts in our bank accounts as your preferred abortion explanation? Can you refrain from waving the influence over our travel plans, our foolishness, or even our time left on earth as your second and so forth defense? I agreed with you, and I don't want to stress over stress anymore either. However, there are absolutely no limits to the amounts of excessive excuses. This is it. It stops here; an abortion, I will never allow. You're her father, and I'm her mother, and I am having our child. I will not put myself, my body, or our daughter through that kind of extreme abuse. Nor will I stand by quietly and accept that you can't accept the fact that something good may become of her.

There are no worries, there are no excuses. She's our daughter, and an abortion would be an unethical sacrifice upon her. We're the ones who choose to practice sexual indiscretion. How could we punish our unborn child for our frequent acts of recklessness? We're both equally responsible for her. We both ignored the consequence of having repetitive unprotected sex. Have faith. I know you believe when your daughter is born, your entire world will fall victim to all kinds of inadaptable changes. But once you witness her smile, it won't be very long before she shows you the happiness that your heart embraces and maintains.

Excuse me, w-what are you doing? Wait a minute, where are you going? Are you seriously trying to entertain us at a time like this with music? Yes? Yes, I do indeed need for you to turn that radio back off while I'm trying to finish discuss…wait, you knew that was our song. Wait…stop, I don't want your rich lips kissing me on my skin, nor do I want your tongue lingering in my ear. Okay…all right, that's enough, what about…You are aware that I am unable to resist your hands rubbing all over me like this. Stop, you're turning me on. I can't resist you. Take me. I'm a casualty due to my sexual disadvantage.

Giving…receiving…giving…receiving, his body shivers, my muscles ache, as his manhood simultaneously throbs. Giving… receiving…giving, our message of practicing safe sex has yet again been set aside. Receiving…giving…receiving…giving, his passion, I trust that he no longer wants to prolong our untimely predicament. Receiving…giving…receiving…his answer, he reveals our child of passion will soon be born into this world without fears or resentments.

Looking into Time

➤————❤————➤

Time heals all wounds, right? At least that's the lesson that Vanity Knightingale will have to test for herself. Her first love, Tayten Williams, the one she dreamt of losing her virginity to, has accidentally waltzed his way back into her life. How in the world could Vanity not see this coming? It had been over nine years since she stood in her kitchen window looking down on him in disbelief. Where had he been? What had he really been up to in all this time? And most importantly, what happened to him after that fateful day, when Tayten looked beaten down and came yelling for Vanity outside of her window? Vanity counts on her girlfriend Jayla to help her make sense of her present situation, all the while wondering what would have become of them if she had allowed Tayten to enter her home back then...

Time Will Tell

I'm looking out of my kitchen window with belonged sadness onto the street. I see him. He's running and breathing heavily. He approaches the end of the street. He's standing on the curb, looking up to where my window sits, and starts yelling my name, "Vanity! Vanity! Vanity!" over and over.

Sickened by his appearance, I quickly tucked myself between the window and the wall, hoping that he would not see any movement behind the sheer green curtains hanging in my window. I didn't move an inch. I was simply staring. Here was the man to whom I was supposed to lose my virginity, standing on the curb outside my window, looking dingy as hell. His tall tee, which I swore was supposed to be white, was gray. His jeans looked as if they'd been slept in for weeks upon weeks. And to top it all off, he looked as if he hadn't had his facial hair or his hair cut and trimmed in several months.

All I could think was, *Damn, has it really been that long since the last time we've seen each other? I've only been home for three days, but we've talked on the phone, night after night, within the year I've been gone. What happened between our last meeting and our last conversation that brings him here, to my window, looking like this? Does he really expect me to let his dingy ass into my home, my womb?*

"Nawh girl," I told myself out loud. "I don't know who he really thinks I am, but this isn't how I remember him or what I expect to see of him." I continued to talk, but I didn't want to warrant a response, so I took slow tiny steps back away from the window. Before I could get out of earshot, I heard him yell, "Vanity, please, Vanity…I know you're up there."

I paused to steal one last glace at him before I walked away horrified.

Now it is nine years later, and my past is bleeding its way back into my life and it's crippling me. I am standing at the bar with my drink, Absolute Vodka, splashed with pineapple juice in one hand and my change from my twenty in the other. Heading back to my table, I turned back to ask the bartender for extra napkins. Turning to walk away again, I see him entering the club. I was dumbstruck. My eyes were fixed upon my…ex.

There he stood: confident, stocky, and looking church-house fresh in the entryway of the club. He must have consulted the *Urban Gentleman Magazine*'s fashion blog, because there he stood dressed in a surf-washed Polo shirt, dark khaki pants, with a vented panama hat covering his head. Tayten Prince Williams was standing across the room, returning my eye contact. He started to walk in my direction; his swag was enveloping the room.

They say time heals all wounds right? Unfortunately in my case, it had not; it only gave way for wider, deeper wounds.

"Girl, he's here," I said quickly when Jayla answered her cell phone.

"What are you talking about, girl? Who is here? Where are you? And honestly, getting a drink never took anybody this long."

"Jayla, you tripping? Put the martini glass down and listen to me…hear me. Tayten Williams is here, at this club, right now. I just saw him. Oh-em-gee, girl, he's about to walk right by me."

"Ooh girl," Jayla said after she gulped the last of her martini. "I'm grabbing our purses and I'll be right there. Don't worry girl, we're leaving the club." Jayla hung up her phone, leaving me standing a few tables over from the bar, pleading with my Lord and clicking my heels like my name was Dorothy from the Wizard of Oz. I found myself chanting, *Lord, I wish I were already home, I wish I were already home.* Outside the club, I was pushing Jayla into my 2019 BMW X6.

I drove as fast as I could. When I reached my home, I ran up the stairs, kicked my Dollhouse Neo pumps into the corner of my walk-in closet, took off my off-the-shoulder minidress, threw it in the hamper, washed my makeup off, and slipped into a soothing silk robe. I turned on the radio beside my bed, hoping that the engaging voice of Carl Thomas would ease my mind, but it wasn't working. I turned it off.

I turned the TV on, but at this hour, all that was on were infomercials and reruns of *Law and Order: Criminal Intent*. I turned the TV off and lay in silence. My mind was racing. Tayten's image kept replaying in my head. I called Jayla.

"*Ello*," Jayla said, sounding as if she wasn't ready for the night to end.

"You sure are chipper at three thirty in the morning," I said with sort of a bitter bite.

"I was having a great time until you saw…"

"Tayten," I interrupted. "I can't believe he walked right by me. I mean, he totally acted as if I were a, a…nobody."

"Well, he only repaid the favor. You did treat him the same way nine years ago."

"Damn, Jayla, I know, but the man was sexy as hell, and I can't get him off my mind. What has he been doing to be able to afford clothes like that? And why did he have to show up at the club tonight?

"Vanity, please don't get mad at me," Jayla said. "But I've been talking to Tayten over the years, I mentioned that we would be at Rumors, and well, he thought that he should see for himself how the years had been treating you. I tried to stop him from coming out, but he insisted that I play along with him. He said that it was time that you had a taste of your own medicine, so I kept my big mouth closed, and *poof*, there he was. Oh, and before you get all rude and stuff with me, I think I should let you know that I gave him your address. Tayten should be arriving in the morning, at your house, around ten o'clock, so get some sleep. I still have some partying to do." Jayla didn't even say bye before she hung up in my face.

My jaw weighed heavily on my toes. I couldn't believe Jayla had given a man I hadn't seen in nine years my address. I would have imagined that Tayten and I had at least a couple of phone conversations first. But no, Jayla went there and gave the man my address. I was upset, but I knew my girl had good intentions. I took a few deep breaths. The clock read 4:35 a.m. I pulled my down comforter over my head and forced myself to go to sleep.

I woke fast. My alarm clock seemed to be beeping louder than it ever had before—8:55 a.m. My eyes were crusty, and my stomach ached. *What in the world is wrong with me?* I thought. *How many drinks did I have last night?* I've never, in all my years, had an Absolute vodka and pineapple juice hangover. Why do I feel like crap this morning? I honestly didn't understand this.

It wasn't until I was brushing my teeth and the doorbell rang that I remembered Jayla telling me that she had given Tayten my home address. I froze, wondering if he would go away if I ignored him, but my wondering was short lived; the doorbell rang again. I pulled on some dark blue sweatpants and a gray tank top and headed to the door.

Through the peephole, I could see Tayten; he was dressed in blue jeans and a cream-colored Polo shirt. I swept my hands through my hair, sighed, and opened the door. Tayten gave me a toothy grin; I frowned.

"What's with the frown?" Tayten said while reaching for me. "I thought you'd be happy to see me after all these years. You're gorgeous. Life has surely been kind to you."

"Tayten," I said, trying to sound frustrated. "I don't know why you decided to show up here, but my last memories of you were not what you would call pretty. I didn't understand the manner in which you appeared outside my window then, and I don't understand the way you're acting by appearing outside my door now."

"Well, if you would invite me in, I might be able to explain all of this."

"An explanation would have helped nine years ago but I'm unsure of what will help today," I said as I opened the door wide to allow Tayten to enter my home.

"That explanation thing goes both ways, I believe," Tayten said as he was walking throughout my home, looking at old photos that I had on display in my living room. "You seem to be doing very well for yourself these days."

"Thanks, I do okay. But how well I do is not the issue. You being here after nine years is, and it's time that you started explaining. What happened to you that night?" I felt my chest inflate out of anger.

"Okay," Tayten said with a sigh. "That night I came to your window calling for you, I had been down on my luck for a while, and I was trying to hide it from you."

"Down on your luck? What in the world does that mean Tayten?" I said with little sympathy.

"Vanity, while you were away, all you talked about was how good things were going for you and well, I kind of fell…off. I knew when you came back home, I was going to have to live up to all those lies I was feeding you. I was determined to show you I was who I claimed to be on the phone while you were gone. So the day that you returned, I hooked up with my cousin Wayne. He picked me up along with a few of his friends, and we drove off selling drugs like crazy. As one sell led to another, it started getting late. I told Wayne that I was ready to be dropped off because I needed to get ready to meet up with you. He convinced me to wait. Wayne said he only had one more stop to make but we never made it to that stop."

"What do you mean you were selling drugs? You never made what stop? That doesn't make any sense. I can't picture you as a drug dealer," I said with an annoyed tone.

Tayten started again." I'm not a drug dealer. I wanted to spoil you, and I needed the means to do so since I lost my job a few months after you left. But anyway, that's beside the point. I agreed to do the last run with Wayne when a car crossed over into our lane and hit us head-on. As you saw, I was banged up pretty bad back then. One of Wayne's friends died at the scene. Everyone else had a few lumps and bruises and minor injuries. The accident was only a couple blocks away from where you were. Like I said, it was getting close to our time, so I ran as fast as I could to get to you. But when I got there…"

"I know, I know," I said "I left you outside, screaming and yelling my name. I didn't know what to think. I felt some sort of betrayal. I felt you were lying to me about something, and I was hurt. I know my reaction to you was vain, but I couldn't believe that you would come to me looking the way you did, all the while expecting me to give up my virginity to you. After that night, I vowed to leave you where you stood and I moved on with my life. You should have told me this over the phone, but I would like to apologize to you for not being there for you back then…I'm sorry."

"It's okay," Tayten said. "I'm here now, and that was nine years ago. I'm over it. I've learned a lot about women over the years. I would like to know if maybe we could give it another try. A fresh start, no lies, no drugs. We'll just be two 'older' lovers getting to where we should have been back then."

Attempting to humble my response I said, "Tayten, we can't make up for nine years just like that. We are two totally different people on two totally different paths. All I can offer at the moment is my friendship, and even that is a super shaky subject indeed."

"You know, Jayla, warned me that getting you back wasn't going to be as easy as I expected it to be, but what the hell, I'm up for the challenge. I was your first love, and you were mine, and I've learned that you don't give up on love. Agree to meet me for lunch tomorrow."

"Lunch tomorrow," I repeated. "Lunch tomorrow…that's possible. Meet me at Wildfire Bar and Grill at 2:30 p.m. We can start our new friendship there. And if you think about standing me up or coming to the restaurant all beat up again, you'd be better off by simply keeping it moving, you hear me?"

"Oh, you don't have to worry. I messed things up years ago, and I refuse to make the same mistake twice. Two thirty, you said, right? I'll be there. Just make sure that you are."

"I wouldn't miss it for the world." I smiled. "But now it's time that you say goodbye. I have a long day ahead of me and frankly, you have taken up way too much of my time already."

"Okay, okay," Tayten said playfully. "I'll leave now, but only because I get to see you tomorrow. Enjoy the rest of your day," he said as he waved and walked back to his car.

I waved goodbye and closed the door. I thought, *What did I just sign myself up for?* Plus, I couldn't believe that after all these years, Tayten still held love for me, even after the way I've treated him. I told myself that I wasn't going to rush things; however, I did rush to inform Jayla of the news of the day.

Turning the Tables

Traditionally when logic and emotion are in conflict, emotion will usually rule the day. But tonight, I decided to tum the tables on that statement and invoke another particular method of reasoning.

"Do you miss me?" he asked.

My stomach clenched. My throat went dry; I had begun to experience a strong agitation of detest. In an instant, I was an emotional wreck; I had to step outside myself.

"Why don't you miss me?" I vaguely heard him say into the phone. I had a choice to make. My response came out slow.

"Well, it's not that I don't miss you. I'm just disgusted. You're not a man of your word, and that's nothing to miss in my book. When I've called you, you haven't answered. I definitely can't miss that," I said sarcastically. "But seriously, your way of making up is very different from mine. I mean, the thought of me driving all the way out there, only for you to think that I was going to have sex with you, after all this time, blew my mind."

"I gave you gas money." He snorted.

"Gas money…Since when does gas money translate to money for sex?" I was livid. I leapt from the dining room chair "You gave me $20. Gas is damn near five dollars a gallon. I know I drive a Suzuki Sport, but $20 means nothing when I drove forty-five miles both ways." I had sweat puddles under my arms. "You know something?" I continued after I took in a deep breath. "I've just decided to stop falling into your emotional traps. You're not of any help to me in any situation. I'm over this conversation and you." I pushed the off button and slammed the phone back into its cradle.

On the table, next to my tall glass of Sutter Home, there was a pack of Djarum Bali Hai filtered clove cigars. I stared at the sky blue, yellow, orange, and green pack, with its lid bent back; I became even more irritated. The pack of cigars that used to come in a box of twenty now came in a box of twelve, and there was only one cigar left in that box. My night couldn't have gotten any worse. I grabbed my lighter and gradually made my way toward the back door that led to the screened in patio.

I lugged an oversized reclining patio chair over to where the moonlight shone the brightest near the edge of the patio. The soft oversized cotton cushions almost devoured me. I flipped, mashed, and, banged until those pastel-pink-and-brown cushions conformed to my irritable body. Shortly after, my body went numb as my mind went to another place. It was like I was dreaming. The images were surreal. I was watching one failed relationship after another play out. And no matter how many times I attempted to turn the relationships in my favor, I kept receiving the raw end of the deal.

Suddenly, a brisk wind blew as a haze swiftly drifted by. I realized I had tears streaming from my eyes. My breathing was rapid, which led to the tightening I was feeling in my chest. This had to be the direct consequence of me losing control over my soul. I continually dated men who were only able to share their penis value with me. I always ended up just being their side fling or their temporary trophy-on-their-arm kind of girl. I believed whatever a man wanted me to believe. I was so caught up; I never sensed that my inner workings were never being stimulated. There was never any substance; majority of the time, I felt…alone.

As the revelations continued to leap out around me like escaping convicts racing toward a common goal, immediately, I was overwhelmed by another surge of dizziness. My legs were heavy, my throat was dry, I could not scream, nor could I cry.

My neck was stiff as a board, I realized when I attempted to sit up. It felt like days had passed, but the reality was, I had only taken a thirty-five-minute nap. Slowly, I eased myself up from the patio chair. I was still feeling a little unstable, but I managed to make my way back through the dining room, to my bedroom at the top of the stairs. I lit two medium-sized pillar candles that I placed at opposite ends of my queen-sized bed. The muscles near the small of my back tightened as I tugged the flat sheet from under my pillows. As I performed that painstaking task, my hand struck my journal, which just so happened to be hidden between the sheets.

I picked the journal up and thumbed through a few pages. My eyes skimmed over a couple of entries before they focused on a section that I had dedicated to Cupid. I couldn't believe what I had written. Within those pages, I could pinpoint exact moments where my logic had wandered off and emotion had come totally into play. I trusted that silly love angle with my most valued part—my heart. I believed Cupid was the bearer of my faith; I had fallen for his phony love spells that made my pretend world harder to escape from. In that moment, I took time to examine myself; I declared that I wasn't going to participate in anymore of Cupid's foolishness. I yanked a pen from the nightstand, plopped down on the bed, turned to a clean page, and then I wrote,

> Dear Cupid,
>
> Can love really keep making me so damn stupid? Since it has, I should be smacking the hell out of you Cupid. Because your choice of men has opened my eyes and revealed unto me that sex objects are all men want, and that's all I'll ever be. For just this last time, I've allowed a man to drag my self-esteem down very low, because his penis was good and I was blinded by its afterglow. Question…how many more disrespectful arrows will you continue to shoot me with? Don't bother to answer that one. Cupid, your last disrespectful arrow left me sick. The next time I'm involved in circumstances that turn out to be the same, I won't prolong the situation, nor will I open my mouth to complain. Particularly because I've learned not to believe man's lame excuses, I won't be playing childhood games or putting up with mental abuse. Cupid, it's time…I'm about to be the one to break your disrespectful chain. I can't keep consenting to men that tarnish my good name. Come out Cupid. It's time that I've confronted you; I'm unaffected

by the amount of pixie dust that you spew. I'm
right here Cupid, and I'm taking a stand; for me
to become a woman, I can't jump to serve man's
every command. I have to take pride in myself
and place my own footprints on top of the sand;
I can no longer depend on you or wait for your
new arrow to land. Cupid, in the past you have
examined me under a desperate light. I can no
longer squint. My eyes have to be wide open in
order not to reenter your hopeless way of life. I
have decided to incorporate and rely on my own
advice. Like a note to self, those lines have been
right in front of me, and those lines on that page
clearly read, "Sex should not be confused as love."
Cupid, please get it right. Ecstasy should last a
lifetime, not merely for one night.

I was drained, but in a good way; the pressure evaporated from
my back. I closed my journal, leaving the pen inside, and placed it
on top of the nightstand. I did a little stretch, rubbed my eyes, and
then swung my legs up onto the bed. I was finally relaxed. As my eyes
were closing, I yawned and let out a sigh of relief. I knew by the time
the sun came up, I would have the strength to continue deflecting
Cupid's misguided arrows. All I had to do was make sure that I kept
my emotions on a tight leash and agree to let logic guide me the rest
of the way.

I rolled onto my left side. As I did, I remembered thinking
a final thought. I knew it would only be a matter of time before
another man would enter my life, but whoever that man would be,
he would understand that I wasn't going to settle or tolerate foolish
behavior. He was going to have to learn to work with me and not
against me in order to make a relationship work. My purpose would
be for him to recognize my inner beauty as well as my outer beauty.
By morning, I knew I was going to be a stronger person; in the end,
discipline would have reaped the biggest reward.

The Eulogy

It's Sunday, a cold night before Halloween, and I'm snuggled up on my couch. Morgan, my one-year-old black Labrador, is sprawled out on the other end of the couch snoring loudly while she's tucked into her bone-printed cover. My hot chocolate made with warm coconut milk, extra large marshmallows, and French vanilla creamer, is still steaming as it sits on the end table closest to the couch. I was attempting to ignore Morgan's snores while also attempting to watch an episode of *Family Guy*. The topic of choice for tonight's episode was domestic violence. Interested, I tuned Morgan out and tuned into the series.

On *Family Guy*, the character who was Quagmire's sister was in an abusive relationship and wasn't seeing anything wrong with that. Her boyfriend mentally, physically, and verbally abused her. Louise and Peter wanted to help, so they turned to Quagmire to see if he could talk some sense into his sister, to make her understand how much danger she was in if she continued to stay with her abusive boyfriend. Now I can't tell you what this episode really had to do with Halloween as a whole. But what I can tell you is that the topic of domestic violence alone is scary enough. As I watched on, I started to reflect.

I have only been on this earth for thirty-four years; I know that's not a very long time, but through those passing years, I've been through some interesting bouts with domestic violence in a handful of relationships myself. So I can empathize with Quagmire's sister on her views of what would happen if she challenged to leave him. She was a broken and scared woman. For the most part, women in that state rarely recover. They are more than likely to stay right where they are until death, or if they do make it out from under the abuse, they tend to become man haters. Like R. Kelly's song says, "One man can make one woman hate all men." I'm guessing that I'm the one in a million whose heart hasn't turned that cold, but my soul is detached. Trust is one the hardest thing for me to give freely to a man—or anyone, for that matter. My thoughts started to fade as the TV sounded on; I reached for my now cool cup of hot chocolate and took a sip.

The episode of *Family Guy* was just about over when I heard a screeching sound in my driveway. Morgan leapt off the couch, letting out a loud hound-like bark. I was trying to get Morgan to calm down, but she kept right on barking louder and louder. All of a sudden, there was hard, rapid knocking on my front door. I wondered what in the world could be happening at this time of night. I went over to the door and looked through the peephole and found that Jayla was on the other side of the door, looking distraught. I swung the door open.

"Jayla," I said, "what in the world is wrong with you? Why are you—"

Before I could finish my sentence, Jayla interrupted me.

"She's dead, Vanity, she's really dead," was all she kept repeating.

"Who's dead? What are you talking about?" I groaned.

"Haleigh." Jayla took a long pause. "She's dead. I can't believe it. She's really dead." She went over and sat on the couch. "He did it, girl. James finally killed her."

"What? I just talked to Haleigh Thursday. She told me that she hasn't messed with the man in over a month. She sounded proud when she told me about her newfound freedom. How could this have happened?"

"I don't know, Vanity." Jayla sighed. "All I know is that the police and one of her neighbors found her in her home dead. She was lying on her kitchen floor. Blood was everywhere. They said that she had been beaten up pretty bad."

"Has her mother been contacted?" I asked. I was trying to stay calm.

Jayla's response came out slow. "Yes…her son and the rest of her family as well. Her mother would like for one of us to read her eulogy at the funeral. I can't do it, Vanity," Jayla said with a pained tone. "I can't read her eulogy." Jayla got up from the couch and started to pace back and forth. Her hands were shaking.

"Please calm down, Jayla," I said after I took in a deep breath. "I'll read the eulogy. Just help me gather up some information. What day is the funeral?" I asked as I sat Jayla back down on the couch.

"Saturday," Jayla whispered. "At that church off Murfreesboro Road. The viewing of the body is at 9:00 a.m., the actual funeral is scheduled to begin at 10:00 a.m., and the wake will be held immediately after at Haleigh's mother's house. Oh, Vanity." Jayla's eyes were filled with tears. "I'm so perplexed by all this. Do you mind if I stayed here on your couch tonight? I'm just too shaken to drive."

"Girl, you know I always have room for you. I have some shorts and T-shirt that you may sleep in, and I'll bring you another cover and a few pillows. We're going to get through this," I said softly before I left the room.

Over the course of the next three days, Jayla and I worked tirelessly on the details of our friend's life. By the time Friday rolled around, I had enough information to write our best friend's eulogy.

At 6:45 a.m. on Saturday, I was up. I still couldn't believe that I had to go to one of my finest friend's funeral. By 8:30, I was ready, kind of; I pulled my hair back into a bun and headed out the door toward my car. In my driveway, I just sat in the car and pictured how many times I had seen Haleigh with black eyes and bruises on her body. Jayla and I used to tell Haleigh that she needed to get away from James, but so many times, Haleigh wouldn't listen to us. She would always say that she loved James, and she had no intent of leaving him, because he loved her too. Now I had to deliver her eulogy, damn…

The church was full of people. Old classmates, relatives, immediate and extended family filled the building from wall to wall. I was a nervous wreck, but I had to do what I had come to do, and it was my turn to speak. I made my way gradually down the aisle before I took the stage; I looked into Haleigh's casket. She was lying there as if she were sleeping. Her lifeless body was beautiful; the makeup artist hid her once bruised face well. It appeared as if nothing had happened to her. I closed my eyes and said a soft prayer for her soul, then I went up and took my place on the stage. I began my speech:

"Good morning, family, friends, and fellow classmates. As I stand before you today, I would have never imagined that I would be attending a funeral where I had to bury the spitting image of myself. My dearest friend and confidante, Haleigh A'lynn Myers, has come here to be laid to rest...Lord, please bless her soul.

"Haleigh was a vibrant woman who was born in Cincinnati, Ohio, in 1978. Her mother, Joleigh Elizabeth McNeal, married her father, Julius Lee Myers, when she was twenty-four years old. Her mother had an elder daughter that was six years old, before she married Haleigh's father. Her name was Bailey Alene McNeal-Martin. When Joleigh and Julius married in 1977, Julius, who was twenty-six, adopted Bailey, and added his last name of Myers to hers. When Haleigh turned six, her parents divorced, citing irreconcilable differences, landing Haleigh, her mother, and her older sister in Warren, Ohio, where I met her.

"Haleigh was a quiet, observant girl in elementary school. She didn't shy away from people. She simply felt that she would speak only when she had something useful to say. But there was something about Haleigh's energy that tended to make people of all ages gravitate to her. Maybe it was her big smile that would always brighten the room whenever one of our classmates would do something that was embarrassing. Or maybe it was her quick and unusual sense of humor. Whatever the case may be, Haleigh was loved, and she was going to make certain that the world showed her just how much they loved her.

"In the summer of 1992, Haleigh and her mother moved to Troy, Alabama, where she met an attractive sophomore named Tyrone Anthony Hilliard. Haleigh and Tyrone were lustfully voted in as the campus's 'cutesiest couple.' And by July 1993, they were blessed with their first child, a bouncing baby boy whom they named DaShawn Antwon Hilliard. The reality of bearing a child at the young age of fifteen quickly set in. Haleigh refused to become a statistic. She vowed that she was going to raise a civilized, highly flavored young man that would have his roots deeply set in value-based activities, whether Tyrone stayed around or not. Unfortunately, one year later, Haleigh learned that Tyrone was not really ready for the responsibility of fatherhood. So in 1996, after she graduated from Goshen High School, in Goshen, Alabama, she and DaShawn packed up and moved back to Cincinnati to live with her oldest sister.

"The move back to Ohio sparked a creative era in Haleigh's life. By the time she was eighteen, she was introduced to poetry. She was well read when it came down to authors such as Maya Angelou, Iyanla Vanzant, and Michael Baisden, but her interest in poetry peaked when a mutual male friend chose to express his interest in her through his flowing words of poetry. His only request to her was that, no matter if she turned him down or not, she had to respond with a poem of her own. And being the crusader that she was, she willingly accepted the challenge. I can remember seeing her hunched over a blue card table, with music playing in the background, while she wrote and crumbled up at least a hundred sheets of paper before she finally accomplished her goal of response. Haleigh eventually gave him her poem, and he was truly blown away by the originality of her words. He told her about a few poetry contests that she should enter. She was reluctant at first, but she did enter them all, as well as won them all.

"In 2001, Haleigh decided to leave Cincinnati and move to Nashville, Tennessee. She was such a brave woman. She knew absolutely no one in Nashville, but she was determined to make the move work. She enrolled in Nossi College of Art in Goodlettsville, Tennessee, where she received her associate's degree in digital arts and photography. She also stumbled across a writing school based out of Connecticut, which led to her to being one of the world's most recognizable authors of all times. She has won five Pulitzer awards and has self-published two books, as well as wrote several award-winning articles in various top-name magazines. Haleigh was all about the multitask. She also went on to become a certified public accountant or CPA and financial advisor with three accounting firms in Chicago, Cincinnati, and of course, Nashville.

"When I think of my friend Haleigh, I often picture myself and how she inspired me with her 'we fall down but we get up' attitude. Haleigh was the foundation of strength. Whenever things got tough, she would always make us stand in front of a mirror, window, or any-

thing that showed our reflection, and we would recite a passage by
Carrie, courtesy of Bethany House, women's shelter, that read,

> We're not strong black women; we're black
> women who learned through the years how to
> endure pain, suffering, and loss. These Things
> didn't make us strong; they made us exception-
> ally tolerant black women. As black women,
> we've got to start encouraging others to define
> us in ways that allow our humanness as women
> to shine through…I'm more than a strong black
> woman.

"After we would recite that passage, we would head off to tackle
and complete our next task with a positive, upbeat, outlook through-
out the remainder of our said missions.

"Although Haleigh never married, she leaves to cherish her
memory myself, her best friend; her only child, DaShawn; her three
sisters: Linda, Bailey, and Ashland; two brothers; Julius and Mathew,
as well as a host of grandchildren, godchildren, nieces, nephews, rel-
atives, and friends. One of Haleigh's favorite quotes was, 'A journey
of a thousand miles begins with a single step' by Confucius. Haleigh
endured every mile and every step to get to where she was. She will be
truly missed and forever loved. I know that I have a seat next to you,
awaiting my arrival, loving you always…your best friend, Vanity."

My eyes were full of tears when I finished delivering Haleigh's
eulogy. By the time I made it back to my seat, the Bluegrass
Underground stars, Mike Farris, and the McCrary sisters were per-
forming their rendition of the gospel song, "Just Got to Heaven
(Can't Sit Down)." I lost it; the tears came out hot and fast. I was
confused. I couldn't believe how short Haleigh's life truly was.

After the funeral, Joleigh approached me in the parking lot.

"Are you going over to the burial site?" she asked as she wiped
tears from her bloodshot eyes.

"No ma'am. I can't watch them put Haleigh in the ground. She was like a sister to me. It would be as if I was being buried right beside her. I'm sincerely sorry, Joleigh. I-I just can't."

"I understand." She paused and looked over her shoulder. "That was a very memorable eulogy you gave about my daughter. You surely stirred up my feelings of sentiments, and I wanted to thank you."

I shook my head and replied, "No thanks needed, Joleigh. She was my friend, and that's how I will always remember her. She was a great influence in my life."

"That's sweet of you to say, Vanity," she said as she looked over her shoulder again. "Looks like everyone is about to go, so…"

I stopped her. "It's okay, Joleigh, I'll be sure to call and check on you." I hugged her tight, then we both went away to our awaiting cars.

I met Jayla at Starbucks. When I got there, Jayla was reading an article about domestic violence on her iPad. I sat down beside her, pulled my iPad out, booted it up, and went to the same website that Jayla was on, then I started to read along. The article alleged that over six thousand families were surveyed and they discovered that 50 percent of the men who battered their girlfriends also abused their children. Researchers in that same article argued that experiencing and observing domestic violence teaches girls that violence equals love—that being loved by someone also means being hit by them. They also noted that girls who grow up witnessing battering are also more likely to be abused as adults. There were also some tips on recognizing the signs of abuse such as if your partner has a bad or unpredictable temper, or if your partner acts excessively jealous or possessive. There was domestic violence hotline numbers listed on the page along with some addresses to shelters, where victims could go to receive the proper help and care that they needed.

Jayla and I read more articles and absorbed all the information we could before I leaned back in my seat and sung out, "I got it, I got it."

"What is it, Vanity? What are you thinking about? Tell me, tell me." Jayla was excited. "Do you have some kind of idea forming or what?"

"Indeed I do, girl. What do you think about starting up a scholarship fund in Haleigh's name? We could focus on high school kids. We could also do seminars that would teach them about domestic abuse and how to deal with it, all the while we'd be honoring our friend's name."

Jayla took a moment to answer. "That sounds like a lot of work, but for a friend like Haleigh, I'd do anything to honor her. I'm in. Where should we start?"

Jayla and I searched for information on how to submit scholarships on several websites before we left Starbucks.

I was relived to be home again. "Today was one of the longest days of my life," I said while I let out a long yawn. All that crying and talk about domestic violence had worn me out. I fed Morgan and let her out in the yard to play while I took my shower. When I got out the shower, I still wasn't feeling better, but for the moment, my state of mind was content. My whole life had been changed in the course of one day. All I knew was that I lost someone to whom I was extremely close to. I would never hear Haleigh's voice again, all because her abusive boyfriend decided to take her life. Friends are far too few to be losing them to such a cause like domestic violence. I knelt before my bed and started to pray. I prayed for Haleigh's family, as well as my own. I prayed for the strength to go on with my life, and I also prayed for the message that Jayla and I sent out to reach its intended audience.

Earlier, I stated that I've been through a lot in a short period of time; I'm a domestic violence survivor, and I urge anyone who has had the slightest inkling of abuse to get out and get help. Life is way too short; good night.

Seasons Change

'Tis' the Season is a story of a woman's struggle after she loses her job, of which she has devoted eight years of her time and services to. She is abruptly thrown into real-life situations: family and relationship problems, the sudden loss of her job, past due bills, and the disturbing feelings of fear as she absorbs the realization that she could be about to lose the roof over her and her dog's head.

The commotion during this time in her life leaves her questioning herself, as well as the actions of others around her. With the holiday season quickly approaching and complicating her with ever more issues, she begins to panic. She is not used to being put in a position where she has to rely on friends or family to help get her through times of hardship; she is spoiled by the so-called finer things in life. She is reluctant at first, but through some deep soul-searching, she uncovers twelve of life's most significant lessons.

By conducting interviews through Facebook in a manner similar to the styles used in the book *Listening Is an Act of Love* by David Isay or Delilah's book *Love Matters*, she accumulates information which will send her on a path to soothing the progression of her unpleasant nervousness. Once she updates her status on Facebook to a simple request for all to partake in posting at least one life lesson a day for twelve days until the New Year arrives, her family and friends encourage her to evaluate herself as well. As she begins to prioritize her own list of twelve life lessons, she begins to recognize the power of unconditional love. She starts to feel a rouse in her emotional state; her physical self has been awakened, and the answers to her prayers have been sitting right in front of her the entire time.

Her story is being told through the blessings and consent from the emotional words of others. She is taken aback, as she notices how the dialogue between the arranged lists of life's lessons she compiles through sources such as Facebook, Twitter, email offer the exchanges of ideas and opinions to be expressed through stories of love, loyalty, honor, and respect. As she grows throughout life's extended journey, she realizes in the end, that there was something beautiful inside of her that made her family and friends love her unconditionally all along, and by publishing her book of twelve life lessons, she understands that she was taught the most valuable lesson of them all: she has to love herself first in order to survive.

'Tis the Season

We must hurt in order to grow. Sometimes our vision clears
only after our eyes have been washed clean with tears.

—Yolanda Mcmillian

I lost my job four months ago. Direct TV has since sent a
return-to-sender box to my address. My electricity bill along with
all my other utility bills are past due. My car note is two months
behind, and to top it all off, my dog decided to chew and shred
my couch pillows this morning. I stared at the mess that had been
created inside of my apartment. It was clear that my personal life
as well as my home life had become disaster areas. Not to mention
the holiday season, which was intended by all to be one the most
joyful times of the year, was swiftly approaching; it appeared that
I was going to be the only one on a train track headed straight to a
place called Low Expectation-Ville. How in the world was I going to
replace a three-thousand-dollar couch or pay my past due bills with-
out any income? I plopped down in the middle of the living room
floor, crossed my legs, put my hands over my face, and started to cry.

I knew this holiday season was going to be the worst one yet. I
called the credit union to check my savings and checking accounts.
The balances were unfortunately low. I didn't even have enough
money to purchase my only child a decent Christmas present this
year. Although there had been times when I had wondered if my
child even deserved a present, because he had been a tad bit more
disrespectful than I would have liked him to have been; I mean, does
taking off in your mother's car without asking and bringing it back
on less than a fourth of a tank away from empty, count when it
comes down to Santa's naughty-or-nice list? I didn't have an answer
for that question, but what I could say was, the good has outweighed

the bad. My son has maintained a college grade point average of 3.75. He has also made it through his third year of living on college campus without turning me into a youthful grandmother. Some may not share my beliefs on these things being viewed as huge accomplishments, but being an African American male these days without a criminal record or kids, alongside holding down a steady GPA in college with a good-paying job, spoke volumes when it came down to the student as well as the parenting skills of his mother. But to be honest, none of that mattered at the moment, I had to do something to create some type of income fast before my dog and I were set out on the curb, chewed couch and all.

Before I could sit down to devise a plan to get myself out of this mess, I had to first clean up the mess around me. I had to struggle a little, as I gradually stood up. My leg muscles had tightened because I'd sat in the middle of the floor for so long. I caught my balance and then went over to open the back door that led to the fenced-in yard. I let Morgan, my dog, out to play. After I closed the door, I proceeded over to the area where all the stuffing from my couch pillows lay. I plucked the giant white cotton balls off the carpet, dusted both of the oversized glass TV stands, vacuumed behind what was left of the furniture, wiped off all the mirrors, made up my bed, rearranged all the perfumes and hair products on my dresser, and emptied out all of the trash cans. Before I knew it, I'd cleaned my entire apartment, and my body was dripping from perspiration. I lifted my left arm and took in a deep whiff; I was unhappily greeted by a foul funk. I quickly dropped my arm back down to my side. I smelled like I had been running from a wild pack of pit bulls. I was in desperate need of a shower.

I pulled my sweaty racer-back tank top over my head, untied my drawstring booty shorts, kicked the clothes into the neat pile that I had left on the hallway floor, and sauntered to the bathroom inside of my bedroom. My stride to bathroom was broken when I heard the reminder alert beeping from my cell phone that sat on the bookshelf in the hallway outside my bedroom door. I grabbed a towel from the hook I placed on the wall between my room and the bathroom and wrapped it around me. I went over to the bookshelf, picked up my

Nokia Lumia 710 Windows phone, and rubbed my middle finger over the touch screen to bring the phone to life. As the screen popped up, I read the calendar reminder message that said, "There were only twelve days left until the New Year arrives." As the phone went back into sleep mode, I stuck my tongue out at it and tossed it on my bed, then I made a beeline back toward the bathroom.

I turned the hot water on for my shower. As the vapors intensified, I placed my face in the path of the steam and let out a long, deep, purposeful growl. I prayed, as the soothing vapors wrapped themselves against my skin. After an extensive period of time, the hot water turned cold. I exited the shower and toweled myself off. I hoped that I would be relaxed enough to figure out a way to lift my spirits and deal with my cash flow problems.

After I completed the ritual of wiping my face with witch hazel, I put on some of Sauvé's Naturals Mango Mandarin body lotion, and sprayed myself with Pink Sugar perfume. The sweet, fruity fragrances in the air were refreshing. I slipped my feet into my plush house shoes that were waiting at the bottom of my bed and went over to check my laptop. I noticed that my Facebook page was still up. I sat down in the desk chair and scrolled through the most recent news feed. It appeared that all my Facebook family and friends were going through some sort of joint venture of frustrations and hardships. All the posts were about either money troubles due to holiday shopping or relationships that weren't working out. As I continued to scroll, I noticed that there were a lot of comments and likes on a particular post that my sister, Lil Momma, posted fifteen minutes prior. The post said, "Only those who embrace the wisdom of common sense shall prevail." I was deeply impacted by that statement. I kept scrolling until I came across another post that read, "As long as I have these three things; faith, hope, and love, you will never break me. —T. King." I had begun to see patterns within the posts. I felt inspired. I scrolled through a few more post before I ended up at my profile status update bar.

The cursor blinked as it waited for me to type out my thoughts. I was in no rush; I closed my eyes and flashed back to the patterns within the posts. I took in a deep breath, opened my eyes, and started to type. Since there were only twelve days left until the New Year, I asked everyone on Facebook to post one life lesson a day on my wall until we reached the year 2013. I stated that I would be the first to start the chain. I posted, "Someone told me that success could be found within my fragments." I clicked the Send button and waited. About five minutes ticked by before I started to get worried. I wondered why no one wanted to comment on this particular subject. I was about to post another message when a notification appeared in the status bar. It read, "Two friends liked your status update." I was a little excited, but that was not enough for me. I wanted my friends to post lessons that they have learned over the years, not simply like my status. I was aggravated.

I was hesitant, but I positioned the pointer over the settings button and clicked. A drop-down menu appeared, and the log-out button was at the top of the list. I was just about to click on it when another notification showed up. This time there was a comment waiting on my status bar. My auntie posted a message that read, "You cannot correct the past or control the future, so the best way to succeed is to do your best in the here and now."

A huge smile spread across my face. I was certain that I was going to receive other wise and encouraging comments. I waited a few more minutes. Another message from my friend PJ came through, which read, "If you don't talk to yourself, others will put you down."

I was overwhelmed; I finally had the support I needed. I stood up too quickly and knocked the chair over. My Facebook family was behind me 100 percent.

I greatly appreciated all the feedback, but evening had begun to set in, and I was hungry and tired. I thanked all those who participated before I logged off; I also updated my status with a reminder message stating that there were still eleven days left until we reached 2013, and I encouraged everyone to keep posting until we reached the New Year. I shut my laptop down and headed straight to the refrigerator.

I was hungry but not hungry enough for a full-course meal. I settled for a quick roast beef, mesquite turkey, and cheese egg sandwich, with a side of fries. The remote was on the table; I picked it up and turned the TV on. I sat down on the end of the couch that wasn't torn up as bad; I pressed the guide button and flipped through the menu until I found the TV1 channel. An old episode of *Martin* was about to start. I placed my plate on a tray and happily ate my food. While I chewed my food, my mind wandered off in the middle of a commercial break. I was thinking about tomorrow. It was a new day, which meant there was going to be a full day's worth of new comments that awaited my responses.

Moonlight

My mouth is still full of blueberry smoke. My lips parted, making the luscious white waves dance around his fully erect penis. The veins in his silky chocolate skin were full and elevated. I smiled devilishly upon his mighty, thick dark sword; I exhaled slowly, releasing the last of the sweet blueberry smoke against the mild night winds. Stabling myself on my knees, I lean over. My mouth is undeniably wet. I drizzled my juices down his engorged shaft. Watching his penis become harder under the moonlight excited me more. I touched my tongue to the tip and started drawing circles. He shudders with pleasure as he grips the center of my thick curly black afro; I'm excited! I place my mouth over his penis until I feel it swell in my throat. I allow him to control the pace and then…

Animals, that is what the noises in the night sound like. He pushes his sword deeper into my shiny pleasure hole. Gasping to the beat of every pump, I fight to gain control. I want him, but I want him on my terms. His rhythm is getting faster, as he's hitting me harder from the back. I moan and attempt to wiggle myself free. My knees are buckling, but I regain my strength. I reach down between my legs. My fingers tap-dance along his slippery shaft that is covered in my warm sticky juices. He continues to long stroke me. He wants the win, but I need the win more. I grab his sword on the out stroke and push myself away. My legs are spaghetti, and my sweet spot is spewing warm streams of pleasure down my thighs. My voice is raspy, but I command him to the ground. His dark eyes are mannish as he looks up and see my thighs twinkling in the moonlight. I take advantage of his dazed state. I lower my body down so his tongue could take his sword's place. He greedily begins to suck and lick me from front to back. I lose control. I explode on his face. Animalistic behavior shows on my face. His grin and beard are glossy under the moonlight. He believes he won round 3, but I still want him. There is still a fighter within me. I move sensually down and fill my sweet sunshine with his sword again. On top, I perform Kegel exercises on his hard shaft until he digs his fingers deep into my hips. I move faster; up, down, side to side. I'm in my zone. He can't fight the feeling. His shaft is pulsating and swelling under the pressure ready to release but then...

At this point, I am on the verge of an emotional fucking TKO. Mentally, I'm lost. My emotions are gushing from my pussy. Physically...physically, I appear to be defeated. His massive sword is attempting to conquer me from the inside, but I will not lose. I am a sexual fighter. I will agree that he is my equal, but not tonight. On this night I shall reign queen. I quickly gather my thoughts, and we change positions. On my back, he slides his sopping wet manhood inside me again. I gasp, making him comfortable enough to drop his guard. Long slow strokes, tip of his head pumps, followed by fast thunder-ish pumps lead him to believe that he...he would be the champion. With one leg spread wide and the other leg wrapped around his back, I changed his rhythm. Slow, deep, and steady, I clench my pussy muscles. His massive sword begins to pulsate inside me. I grip and release. He's ready to erupt. I grip, release, and lightly kiss his chest. I run my tongue up his neck until I find his mouth. Distracted by his tongue dancing with mine, I clench and release my pussy muscles again. On the down stroke, he belts out an enormous roar, thrusting and bucking like a raging bull under the moonlight. Watching him with glazed eyes, I am excited and exhausted. Pressing his sword deep within me one last time, he lowers his head to lie on my chest.

Breathing heavily, I whisper in his ear, "Your show is over. I'm the winner tonight," as I am genuinely smiling under the moonlight.

I'm on Strike!

Yeah, my boy, you can't get no mo' ass.
That's right, you heard me, I'm on strike.
One reason is you always want me to dance, do flips, and twerk for you.
And I don't feel like that's something that I should always have to do.
What happened to the days when you would be rubbin', crestin', and
      trying to turn me on?
Why can't you make love to me or attempt to f——k me good when
      I'm not wearing your favorite thong?
Consequently, until you change and start treating me right,
You can't get no mo' ass, 'cause I'm on strike!

Decisions

Leave, stay, complain, love, or hate?
Here's a few decisions that my mind often fails to contemplate.
For if I make the choice to stay and hate,
How will my creator then, decide my faith?
I can imagine my life with, but not without you.
So stay, no, leave…this is bullshit, I still can't figure it all out, I'm so
damn confused.
Oh wait, I've got it, I'll just stay and complain.
Oh hell no, did I just hear myself, am I not right in the brain?
I know that we would not survive our love story, like that. For us,
that would be like setting up a pay-per-view to watch a Roy
Jones Jr. versus Mike Tyson in a match on Saturday night fights.
With that being said, I see that there's only one choice left for me to
choose.
And this could be the choice that leaves a small footprint on my new
blue suede shoes.
In my heart, this choice feels like something that should be shared
unconditionally.
This choice is something that supports you mentally as well as
physically.
This choice is something that comes from my creator above.
This choice is a 4-letter word, this choice is L.O.V.E.; it's love (I sing
in my Jill Scott voice).
I will choose to stay and love you because we have come too far to live
out our lives through stereotypes.
You are my lover, my man, my entire world, can't you see.
I'm pleading, hoping that you'll listen, feel, and comprehend me.
You are my soul, my breath, my most respected friend on this hectic
place that we call earth.

I feel love will cast its light over us and send our souls into a state of
    rebirth.
I'm pleading, I hope you're listening, I need you to feel me and
    understand.
That I stand on this decision, as your one and only stoic woman.

Heinous Crime

Love is such a heinous crime
Love is a word just said over time.
Love is like a big race
And at the end, you get smacked in the face.
'Cause everything you do will come back around,
Then your heart will be left, stomped, dead, lying on the ground.
Love is a word that's supposed to be blind
But if it was, would it be such a heinous crime?
And if love is a word that's supposed to make you glad,
Then why is it associated with actions that makes you feel bad?
Is it because when you say the word love, it can get you into something like a great big deal,
Like a ride on a roller coaster, called weakness, a cheap thrill.
See, the word love can be said without any remorse,
That's why it can easily be said during the parade leading up to intercourse.
Love is just another 4-letter line,
But it's number one when it comes to heinous crimes.

Colored White Girl

Colored white girl, when you hear the name.

Instantly questions pop into your brain; have they finally lost it?
Did the jump off the deep end suddenly come?

There is no such thing until you look at us, two different races
and one friendship, combined to form a unified bond…*the colored
white girl!*

We do not discriminate because we have animosity toward
everyone. No, fuck that. We hate everyone. But at the same time…

We try to accept what we can't understand. And what we don't
understand is the people who try to hold us down.

Now you say…

How can she fit into the white business world because she has
been "ghetto-ized"?

And how can she understand anything about soul because she
she's…well…pasty?

We yell out into the world, "Please doubt us," because it fuels
the fire to prove everyone wrong.

Don't patronize us by praising our efforts, then laugh behind
our backs.

Have the nerve to laugh in our face, so when we make it, we can
do the same to you, who will still be at a dead-end job, with no plans
to change or upgrade.

The biggest victory is exceeding beyond our own expectations.

And we pray that you never give up on the most important
person…yourself!

As we continue to live our lives in unison or apart, however,
wherever, and whenever, we both know that *colored white girl* is
reflective *now and forever*.

The Man I Want

Before, if you'd asked me, I would say that I didn't know what I wanted in a man before today.

'Cause I've been through a lot of relationships you see, that's how I discovered what the one should be.

The first thing on my list, I must say, is that my man has to have his head on the right way.

There are other qualities in a man that I want too, if I may, may I continue?

I want a man who keeps it real.

A man who doesn't only let God know what he feels.

I want a man who kisses and cuddles.

A man who likes to take hot baths, in candlelight, and with bubbles.

I want a man who will tell me sweet things without me asking,

Even when we are not having fun, playing love games, and laughing.

I want a man who is filled with vigor and passion, that to him I'm is never-ending main attraction.

A man who romances my personality with his sexual and unusual ways.

A man who believes my love will always amaze.

I want a man who will stand behind me ten toes strong.

A man who will be there no matter the obstacle course our love goes on.

A man who will trust me without a shadow of doubt, even on the nights that I choose to go out.

I want a man who doesn't interpret sex as just letting him slide it in between, as well as a man who doesn't mistake my passion in conversations as aggressive or me being mean.

I want a man who can stimulate me with his words from afar, that when he hears my voice it's like he wished for me upon a shooting star.

I want to get aroused by every word that my man might say, a man who desires never turns me off or pushes my love away.

A few more things that the man I want must be, he must understand the word WE.

Do unto me as I would do unto he and don't try to control me because true love is free.

Enough said, I'm closing this chapter, and shutting this door, yeah, I know there's more things in a man that I want, that I need to explore.

As for now, I'm leaving behind this segment to work on other pieces of my mind. I'll leave the rest for my soulmate to cultivate and define.

The Letter

I was contemplating for a long time about what type of words that I should put between these lines.

Then like a lightning bolt, it came to me as clear as can be, I'm fed up with the way that you have been treating me.

Why is it that after a certain length of time, I feel like I'm starting to be erased from your mind? When I do talk to you, you proceed to tell me that I'm not in your way, but you stand me up, like every other day.

What is the purpose of your misleading actions? Am I not living up to your satisfaction?

I'm starting to believe that this relationship was built strictly on sex appeal and you're too much of a cowardly punk to let me know that my thoughts are becoming real.

I'm also tired of having to compete for your time, even though you tell me that I'm the only "fine" female in line.

But it's funny, because if that statement is so damn true, why don't you answer your phone when I know that you see that I'm calling you?

Love has to be a word that you just learned, keep using it for play; boy, you will get burned.

I truly don't believe that you care about my emotional pain.

It's obvious because lies still spill out of your mouth like thundering rain.

With fright, your tongue cuts me deep and the word love hits my heart like a sharp dart. I can honestly say that your web of lies is like viewing a priceless work of art.

I fear you because your love is irrational and unclear. The only time that you ever reveal that you love me is when you're drunk off Remy, D'usse, or Budweiser beer.

What in our situation made your actions towards me change? And why are you choosing me to be the star of these stupid-ass mind games?

Why can't you open your eyes to see that I've never been fake to you nor have I've been a gold-digging honey? I wanted you for you, not your car, sex, or money.

The only thing within these lines that I wish that you could see, is that your lies, well, they are hurting me.

I understand that that's awfully hard for a fuck boy like you to understand. But you may try to holla back at me when that little boy inside you grows up and becomes a man.

Until then, here are a few choice words that I'm sure that you can comprehend, because these four words came strictly from you. I learned them and now I'm turning your words back around and I'm using them on you.

Gone on ahead, boy, and "do what you do." I'm out of here, I've found better things to give my focus to.

I refuse to keep living within this dreadful light. I can no longer keep attempting to win and lose this imaginative fight.

I Come to Thee

It may seem that I have everything
But to me, all I have is agony and pain,
I hope my love for the other will stop this drowning rain.
Trapped is the way that I feel,
because I have no idea which way my love will spill.
Both relationships started with the same potent script,
but now, the other is the one that I would like to share the rest of my
    life with.
I'm yearning to put the first relationship in the past but it's such a
    hard thing to do,
because the first helps me with my son and he wants a child of his
    own too.
But how I feel about the other, I know that he is right for me in every
    way.
I can't get him off my mind, I feel his love with me every step of my
    day.
I know I shouldn't feel like this and it is a shame, I must say,
because I know my love for the other will only push my first love
    away.
As my mind swirls, I drop down to my knees to pray.
I ask you, Lord, to guide me, lift me, and push me the right way.

Self-Advice

Have you ever met someone so focused, so kind, who is willing to share a future with you without any lies?

Have you ever met someone who is so outspoken and straight to the point, that he could light your interest, instead of the end of his joint?

Have you ever met someone with deep, dark, innocent eyes, that when you look into them, you know that there are no feelings being kept bottled up inside?

Have you ever met someone who encourages you to go after your dreams in life, that if you made a left, he would help you make a U-turn to make it right?

Girlfriend, listen, here's a bit of self-advice: if you were to ever run into a man that displays this kind of style and spice.

Run away with him girl, don't think twice. Run away with him honey, go on ahead and start your new life.

But make sure that you keep in touch with your family and friends; write them, call them, email them every now and again.

Oblige him. Let him know that you are a strong Black Sista. Convey to him that you'll always have his back. Revel to him that you have character and you know when, how, and where to react.

This next part is the most important piece of self-advice: make sure that you truly want your new life.

Make sure that you don't lose touch with yourself. Make sure that it is your life, not his, that is living and breathing within in your every breath.

For then, Sister, as you have started to settle down inside your new life, you will be able to add new things to your already long list of self-advice.

To Leave or Stay

Are you an illusion? Your actions brought me to this abrupt conclusion. You have me caught in a web with your contradictory ways. Shit, N!##@, what's it going to be? Leave or stay?

One minute, I'm your baby girl living in a fantasy world. The next minute, I find myself looking for love in all the wrong places. I'm sitting back wondering how our relationship all of a sudden came apart like shoelaces.

But what I genuinely can't seem to understand is, if we are supposed to be finding out what love is for us, why are you suddenly deciding to trade our love in for bust?

I thought that in a relationship, two people learned how to compromise. To me, that means I won't fill your head with lonely cries. I won't be disrespectful or unfair to you, and I won't even agree with every plan that you stew.

What I will do is keep dry eyes because the feelings we share will continue to keep me warm and fuzzy inside. I will tell you everything will be okay as we work together to better our lives each and every day. And to even avoid an argument with you as my man, I will learn to agree to disagree with some of your flimsy plans.

So I ask you…to leave or stay? It is your decision.

If it is to stay, we can resume our lovemaking mission.

If it is to leave, you won't ever have to worry about me again. In the end you will know, that you passed on a virtuous women.

About the Author

As an author, Tricia "Reighn" Davis is a voice. A voice that speaks particularly through intuition and reasoning. A voice that broadens views through poetry and snapshots of life. She has found her voice, and she is blessed and thankful to be sharing her voice with you, her readers.

Originally, Reighn is from Cincinnati, Ohio. She moved to Nashville, Tennessee, at a young age and found her voice by answering a letter from a writers' program based out of Wilmington, Delaware. Through many courses, she was determined to craft her skills, she evolved, and published her first book. Her characters and storylines mimic life. Distinct situations take the reader on a journey throughout each phase, allowing you, as the reader, to place yourself within each story line on every page.

Reighn is inspired by life revolving around her. Her intentions are to remain relevant as well as relatable through the creative process of observing, visualizing, and writing. As she uses her voice to teach, reflect, empower, and uplift, she continues to gain knowledge and insight into the world in which she, a stoic woman, was built.

Based out of Antioch, Tennessee, writing is her lifestyle that she adores with a passion. By harmonizing poetry and short stories, she synchronizes emotions and reality, which places the reader on an adventurous, thrilling ride. As stated in the beginning, Reighn is a voice, and her gratitude toward her readers is unmatched as well as appreciated, and she would like to thank all her readers in advance for their continued love and support.